Leadership Lessons
for Coaches

Leon,
You're a great blessing - I've
enjoyed seeing you develop
into a great young man
of God -
Hope to see you on FCA
staff soon —

Sid Callaway

Ps. 84:11

Leadership Lessons
for Coaches

Sid Callaway

POWER PUBLISHING
Incorporated

Leadership Lessons for Coaches

Sid Callaway

Editor: Susan Andres

ISBN-13: 9780984287413
ISBN-10: 0984287418

Power Publishing
13680 N. Duncan Drive
Camby, IN 46113
(317) 347-1051

This book is manufactured in the United States of America.

Library of Congress Control Number: 2009941357

Published by Power Publishing
13680 N. Duncan Drive
Camby, IN 46113

Exterior and interior layout by Carol Anne Hartman

Contents

Acknowledgments		vii
About the Author		ix
1.	That You May Believe	1
2.	Good Habits Raise Effectiveness	3
3.	Preparation	5
4.	Planning	7
5.	Time Management	9
6.	Mission Success	13
7.	Standing Firm	15
8.	Thankfulness	17
9.	When the Going Gets Tough	19
10.	Resolution	21
11.	How Can I Still Win in Defeat?	23
12.	Lead, Follow, or Get Out of the Way	25
13.	Decisions	27
14.	Whom Do You Learn From?	29
15.	True Leaders	31
16.	Leaders Never Quit Learning	33
17.	Prepared for Competition	35
18.	Responsibility	37
19.	Insight	39
20.	Achieve	41
21.	Responsibilities	45

22.	Inadequacy	47
23.	Qualities of a Leader	49
24.	Rebuilding	53
25.	Types of Leadership	55
26.	Authority	57
27.	Team	59
28.	Failure	63
29.	Praising	65
30.	Character	67
31.	Values	69
32.	Improvement	71
33.	Connect	73
34.	Daddy	77
35.	Priorities	79
36.	The Urge to Quit	83
37.	Intentional Leaders	85
38.	Consistency	87
39.	Future	89
40.	Leadership Qualities	91
41.	A Good Name	93
42.	Advice to Young Leaders	97
43.	Keep Growing	99
44.	Leadership Requirements	101
45.	Influence	105
46.	Giving Your Best	107
47.	Growth	109
48.	Risktakers	111
49.	Commitments	113

Acknowledgments

I am most thankful to my family—LuAnn (my wife of twenty-eight years who is a professional counselor in private practice) and my son, Jacob (20 years old and a soldier in the U.S. Army). They are a great inspiration to me.

Thank you also to my parents and to the many people (too many to name) who have poured into my life. But most of all, I am most grateful to my Lord and Savior Jesus Christ for life, salvation, and giving me the ideas for this book.

I also want to thank Susan Baughcum for all the hard work she did on this project. She ran my professional life for 4 ½ years, and even though she has moved away, she still helps me with several Fellowship of Christian Athletes (FCA) projects.

A special thank you to R V Brown who has been there for me over the years as my leader, accountability partner, best friend, and one who is closer than a brother.

And finally, thanks to Coach Arthur Hawkins who is a true example of a leader in every way. He is a great friend who could never be replaced.

I couldn't have done this without my FCA teammates. You are a great blessing to me.

Note: All scripture quotations, unless otherwise indicated, are taken from the New King James Version Bible. Copyright 1979, 1980 by Thomas Nelson, Inc.

About the Author

Sid Callaway is a 17-year employee of the Fellowship of Christian Athletes (FCA) in the Atlanta, Georgia area. He is a former walk-on football player at the University of Georgia. As a hobby, he is a certified strength and conditioning coach. Sid has appeared as a guest several times on TotaLee Fit, Lee Haney's (8 – Time Mr. Olympia) television show on TBN.

Week 1

That You May Believe

Game Plan:
John 20:30–31

Challenge:

This is why the gospel according to John was written—that we might understand that Jesus is God in the flesh and that we can have a personal relationship with him.

The word *believe* in the Bible is a powerful word. It means, "to acknowledge the truth as truth; and that I accept the Person of Jesus Christ into my life." My definition is "to commit to with every fiber of your being."

It is a total sell out—all our eggs must be in one basket, no reserves, no safety net, no holding on to any other options. In the same way, we must believe in what we are doing. It is more than just athletics. It is making a difference for all eternity. If you, as a leader, have not bought into this total commitment, you cannot effectively influence anyone else to do so.

Pursuit:

1. Do you have a personal relationship with Jesus Christ?

2. What is your commitment level?

3. What is keeping you from total commitment?

— Sid Callaway —

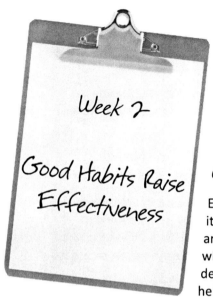

Week 2

Good Habits Raise Effectiveness

Game Plan:
James 1:22,
Ephesians 5:1–2

Challenge:

Everyone has habits. Some habits are good, some not so good, and some are just bad. People who are not disciplined fail to develop the good habits that are helpful for them to be successful.

The Apostle Paul was a disciplined Christian. Not only was he a great leader in his day, but also his leadership continues to this day. He set a great example in so many areas, for example, in commitment, perseverance, mentoring, persistence, faithfulness, mental and physical toughness, and in many more areas. So, I have been thinking about ways good habits can raise our level of effectiveness. Here are a few:

✓ *Daily Bible reading and prayer.* These are necessary. God made us for a purpose, and His plan is given to us. So, we must read it and discuss it with Him daily.

✓ *Repetitive reading.* It is a good habit to read certain things almost daily. I read "My commitment as a Christian" and other things almost every day to keep my focus. A good thing to read regularly is the Competitor's Creed of the Fellowship of Christian Athletes (FCA).

— *Sid Callaway* —

✓ *Encouraging people.* Effective people encourage others regularly. Even if you are the one that needs encouragement, still reach out to others.

✓ *Balanced life.* Stay balanced. Eat, sleep, and exercise right. Our minds are sharper when we are balanced.

✓ *Hobbies.* A good habit is to have a project or hobby that is unrelated to our vocation.

✓ *Priorities.* It is definitely a good habit to keep our priorities in order. President Abraham Lincoln's son could meet with him anytime, no matter what important business the president was attending to.

✓ *Giftedness.* Successful people know how they are gifted and spend most of their time operating in their particular gifts. Someone once said, "Do what you do best, and delegate the rest."

✓ *Growth.* A good habit is to keep on growing. No one has arrived.

Pursuit:

1. Make a list of your habits. Are they helping you become an effective leader, or are they disabling your leadership role?

2. Are you balanced in your spiritual and physical lives?

3. Are your priorities in order? Where does your family fit in your daily walk?

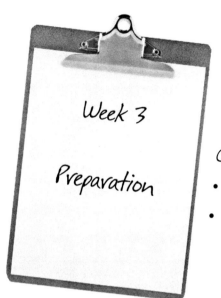

Week 3

Preparation

Game Plan:
1 Samuel 17

Challenge:

- Training makes the difference.

- Games are won or lost on the practice field.

I heard someone say once that players win games. That is true, but coaches train the players, motivate the players, enable the players, give example to the players, educate the players, and add value to the players.

I like the quote by John Wooden, "When opportunity comes, it is too late to prepare." The famous saying "we play like we practice" is so true. I know we get up more for games, but the time spent in preparation is vital.

Many people read the story of David and Goliath in 1 Samuel 17 and think David just showed up one day and fought Goliath and defeated him. That is not exactly true. God spent years preparing David for this event. David's years in the wilderness (that was his practice field) prepared him spiritually, physically, and mentally for this battle. We know that David won, but he won because of the Lord.

You must keep preparing yourself so that you can prepare your team for the "game"—their walk with Christ. Together with God as your trainer, you, too, will win the battle.

— Sid Callaway —

Pursuit:

1. Are you leading your team, or is your team leading you?

2. How are you preparing yourself and your team for the task ahead?

3. Are you spending time in prayer seeking out His plan for you and your team?

Week 4

Planning

Game Plan:
Nahum 1:7

Challenge:

I know that planning is important to coaches. It should be important to everyone, but coaches have so much to plan for in their jobs. When you sit down to plan your school schedules, team schedules, practice schedules, and your personal schedules, do you try to discern what God wants?

If we do not seek God in our plans, we can easily become discouraged. When we do not seek God's plans first, then our focus is on ourselves. Then, when things do not go as planned, we blame others and ourselves, and we get depressed and discouraged. Dr. Stanley said, "Discouragement blinds us." When we dwell on our disappointments, we become discouraged.

However, when we recognize that God is in control and when we follow Him daily, we can handle the bad times. This is because whatever happens has to run past God before it gets to us. When we realize that God knows what is going on, we can be encouraged even in tough times. We can even be an encouragement for others. While going through one of the toughest times in my life, I was able to help and encourage a friend going through a tragedy in his life.

I want to encourage you to hang in there, even if it is one minute at a time. Let God know how you feel. Let Him be your focus. When He is our focus, our attitude changes.

— Sid Callaway —

Pursuit:

1. Have you put God first in your planning?

2. Are you following God daily, through the good and the bad?

3. Is your focus on Christ or on your current situation?

Week 5

Time Management

Game Plan:
Ephesians 5:15–17

Quotable Quotes

Time is Opportunity.
—Dr. Charles Stanley

When opportunity comes, it is too late to prepare.
—Coach John Wooden

Coaches seem to be the best at time management. With hectic schedules and many things to juggle, they have everything timed to a science. I have been to so many practices and seen this repeatedly. Warm-ups are given a certain amount of time; drills and scrimmages are timed to the second. I suppose it has to be that way if you are to get everything done that you set out to do.

If we are to be successful, we have to make time, plan, and set goals for success. Ephesians 5:15–17 talks about redeeming the time because the days are evil. Wasting time is a sin. So, time is important.

— Sid Callaway —

9

Some Thoughts on Time Management:

- ✓ We are responsible for how we spend our time.

- ✓ "I don't have enough time" is no excuse. Everyone has the same amount of time. We may choose not to do something, because other things are more important.

- ✓ Good organizational skills will help us not waste time.

- ✓ Ask the Holy Spirit for guidance.

- ✓ We will all run into detours. Do not let them wreck your day. Change, regroup, and continue on course.

- ✓ Get rid of distractions.

- ✓ Focus on your strengths. Focusing on your weaknesses takes too much time.

- ✓ Let those around you help with schedules and timing.

- ✓ Review how you spend your time regularly.

- ✓ Most importantly, do not leave God out.

Pursuit:

1. Are you leading your schedule, or is your schedule leading you?

2. Do you have a plan to keep your schedule in order? If not, find someone or something that can help you.

3. Are you leaving God out of your day?

Week 6

Mission Success

Game Plan: John 14:6

Challenge:

All leaders are on a mission. This is critical for success. To be successful at our mission, we must do the following:

✓ *Know our mission.* It is great to be on a mission, but are we on the right mission? A great game plan for the wrong team is no good.

✓ *Embrace our mission.* Once we know our mission, we must believe in it. We cannot sell it if we do not believe in it.

✓ *Communicate the mission.* Our team must know the mission and buy into it. When we communicate our mission effectively, we are essentially giving it to our team, so they can be successful.

God has a plan, purpose, and mission for our lives. He has communicated it to us through His word, pastors, His Holy Spirit, circumstances (good and bad), and through others.

Our success in life depends on how well we buy in, accept, and live out this mission. Jesus said in John 14:6, "I am the way, the truth, and the life. No one comes to the Father except through me."

— Sid Callaway —

13

Pursuit:

1. Do you know your mission, and do you believe in it?

2. Have you communicated your mission to your team? Are they committed with you?

3. Are you living out your mission?

— Leadership Lessons for Coaches —

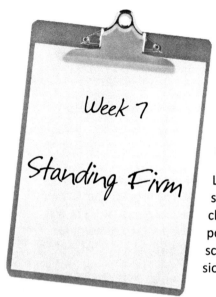

Week 7

Standing Firm

Game Plan:
Ephesians 6:10–18

Challenge:

Leaders must learn how to stand firm. We are constantly challenged and not always in a positive way. So many people scrutinize us for so many decisions.

In Ephesians 6:10–8, we are encouraged to put on the whole armor of God. The armor is compared to the battle clothing worn by the Roman soldier. In Verse 15, we are told that our feet must be shod with the preparation of the gospel of peace. The Roman soldier had to have on good boots with soles that would not slip because he had to stand firm and hold the battle line.

Here are some ways we can stand firm:

1. *Purpose your heart.* Decide how you will handle certain situations, and stick to it. In Daniel 1:8, he purposed in his heart that he would not defile himself. He did not even give in to the king's orders. Make up your own mind.

2. *Keep focused.* It will be tough under extreme pressure, but we must!

3. *Learn to discern.* Many wrong things seem right. God will help us if we ask Him. Also, we need our own personal board of directors (accountability group) to help us discern.

4. *Do not quit!* I love the quote by Tim Bach: "Everybody hurts, not everybody quits."

Consider the life of Joseph. He was hated by his brothers, sold into slavery, misunderstood, falsely accused, put into prison, and forgotten. However, the Bible says that God was with him. Eventually, he was remembered, given favor, set free, and promoted. He went from "the pit to the palace."

Remember Romans 8:31, "If God is for us, who can be against us?"

Pursuit:

1. What are you being challenged with in your life today?

2. Are you prepared with the armor of God?

3. Are you focused on God and His plan—or have you quit?

Week 8

Thankfulness

Game Plan:
John 19:10–11

Challenge:

To be effective leaders at the highest level, you must be thankful! I hope we all realize that all authority is allowed by God. Jesus told Pilate that he could have no power over Him unless it was given to him by God.

If we are thankful people, then we are not so focused on ourselves anymore, but we realize that it is by much grace and favor that we have a position of leadership.

It is a good idea to reflect often on those we need to be thankful to. Below I have listed a few, but you can add to the list as you choose:

1. *God.* He made us for our mission.

2. *Co-workers.* These are our teammates. We are not in this thing alone. We need others.

3. *Those we lead.* This is why we are leaders—to lead others. What a blessing—it is about service.

4. *Friends.* We need friends who are honest enough with us to point out our blind spots.

5. *Family*. We need a place of safety and refuge. We need to be unconditionally accepted. Yes, we need a cheering section.

6. *Critics*. They may be negative, but even critics serve a purpose—to help us focus.

7. *Mentors*. Whether it is someone we meet with and learn from or a pastor whose tape we get, an author whose book we read, or someone we watch from a distance.

Living a thankful life will cause us to be more humble, and humility goes a long way.

Pursuit:

Make a list today of those you need to express your gratitude to for their faithfulness and service.

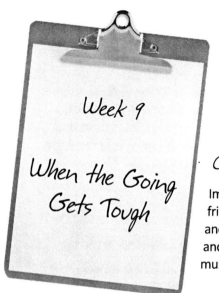

Week 9

When the Going Gets Tough

Game Plan:
Ephesians 6:10–18

Challenge:

Imagine a chase—not your friendly competition. Satan and his demons are chasing us, and we have several choices we must make.

✓ We can turn and fight—us alone against the forces of evil.

✓ We can keep running/riding.

✓ We can give in. After all, temptation looks good at first, and giving in once or twice may not be so bad.

✓ We can become discouraged, even to the point of depression.

✓ We can realize the truth:

- We are at war.
- The forces of evil are too strong to over-come alone.
- We do not have to give in. It is our choice.
- Discouragement is from the devil. God gives us hope.

— Sid Callaway —

There is a war going on. Jesus Christ defeated Satan through His death, resurrection, and ascension. We can live our lives with His power because with His blood, He paid our debt.

Satan is after all those who belong to Christ to make them ineffective. Satan is out to keep those that belong to Christ, so he can destroy them. Satan is especially out to get the leaders in God's kingdom, those on the front lines making a difference for the kingdom of Christ.

We must do the following:

1. Pray without ceasing.
2. Put on the full armor of God daily (Eph. 6:10–18).
3. Summons the angels of heaven to war on our behalf against the demons of hell.
4. Accept the cleansing power of the blood of Jesus and be washed clean.
5. Be accountable. Have lots of fellowship.
6. Admit our weaknesses. Get help where and when needed.
7. Walk in the power of our Risen Lord.

Pursuit:

1. Are you being attacked? Are you joining forces with Jesus Christ, or are you going it alone?

2. Are you taking time for fellowship with other believers, to encourage and uplift you?

3. Where are you weak? Give that to God.

— Leadership Lessons for Coaches —

Week 10

Resolution

**Game Plan:
2 Cor. 5:17**

Challenge:

It is amazing to hear about and even see the New Year's resolutions that so many people make. Gyms are full in January, diet books are bought by the masses, and people make commitments to do so many different things. A new year, commitments, approach to life, and all sorts of things that we consider new are only good if they last.

The best way to become "new" is to accept Christ as your personal Savior and Lord. If you are already saved, you can turn to Him anytime, about anything, to confess any sin, and to be forgiven, cleansed, and become new.

Another bit of good news is that you can do any of this at any time. You do not have to wait until a new year; now is always a good time to do business with God.

Here are more verses to consider:

Ezekiel 11:19: "And I shall give them one heart, and put a new spirit within them."

John 13:34: "A new commandment I give to you, that you love one another, even as I have loved you, that you also love one another."

Revelation 21:52: "And He who sits on the throne said, "Behold, I am making all things new.""

Pursuit:

1. What business do you need to do with God? What do you need to give over to Him?

2. What will you do to help you keep your commitment to Him?

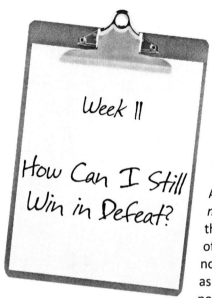

Week II

How Can I Still Win in Defeat?

Game Plan:
1 Peter 1:16

Challenge:

A line from the movie, *Remember the Titans*, that I have thought about, came from one of the players. He said, "We are not perfect as individuals, but as a team we can be." At this point in the movie, they were undefeated as a team even though people on the team had made many mistakes during the course of the season.

We are definitely going to make many mistakes during the course of our lives. Everyone knows this. The question is "How can we still win"? I believe the answer lies at least somewhat in taking some of the following actions:

1. *Building a team around ourselves.* We must have a great team in place to complete us.

2. *Handling temptation.* Proverbs 1:10: Do as Joseph did—run!

3. *Avoiding or getting rid of bad habits.* It is hard just to stop something. We need to replace bad habits with good ones.

4. *Trusting God.* Or just believe God is out there somewhere but involved in our lives. (Believe me; God is completely involved.) We must continually yield to Him. When we cannot, He can. It is hard but keep telling yourself that you can trust Him.

— Sid Callaway —

I hope and pray that we can all win (God's way) in the game of life. Even though we must face great adversity at times, we must keep getting stronger.

Pursuit:

1. Have you built the right team around you?

2. Is temptation dragging you to defeat, or are you running as Joseph did?

3. What is your trust factor level? Do you believe God is all about your life?

— Leadership Lessons for Coaches —

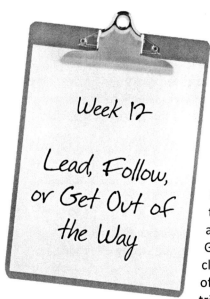

Week 12

Lead, Follow, or Get Out of the Way

**Game Plan:
Ephesians 3:12–14**

Challenge:

One morning when I got up to go for a run, it was raining, and I decided to go to Gold's Gym for the bicycle RPM class. This is forty-five minutes of hard work. The instructor tried to kill us. Every time I do this workout, I have to think of other things to make the time go faster.

So, I began picturing myself racing in open country with mountains in the background. I then pictured myself breaking away from the pack and getting far ahead of the others. (This was only in my mind!) Then, I realized that leaders must come to a point in their lives when they break away from those not going anywhere, from those going in the wrong direction, and from those holding them back.

If you watched the movie, *Seabiscuit*, it was amazing how that horse would get a place in the race when he would look at the horse next to him and take off in another gear to outrun all the others. Joseph had to break away (not by his own choosing, but God works that way sometimes) from his brothers to achieve God's plan for him, his family, and his nation. Gideon had to send most of his army packing to win the battle facing him. Moses had to leave Egypt and the lifestyle he knew to become one of the greatest leaders in all history.

— Sid Callaway —

Glen Cunningham broke away from all the other runners to run the first four-minute mile. He then held the world record in the mile race from 1934 – 1937. I might note that his legs were severely burned when he was ten years old. So, leaders must break away. But then, true leaders begin taking others with them. Real leaders do not share the victory alone. They realize that it takes a team.

Pursuit:

> Do you have people you need to break away from—those not going anywhere, or in the wrong direction, or someone holding you back?

— Leadership Lessons for Coaches —

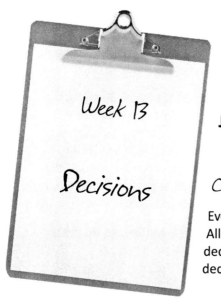

Week 13

Decisions

Challenge:

Everyone makes decisions. All leaders make frequent decisions. Many times, these decisions affect many lives.

A few thoughts about decision making:

1. We must make a decision; we cannot stay neutral. For example, if we need a new car and go to a car dealer, we buy a new car, or we do not, based on the decision we make.

2. When making important decisions, we must not be angry, tired, or hungry. In other words, if possible, be at your best when making life-affecting decisions.

3. The decisions we make today will affect our tomorrow.

4. We are responsible for the decisions we make. I remember a college student saying he decided to have premarital sex just one time. As a result, he will carry disease with him to his grave.

5. "Our decisions can override God's plan for our lives," (Ike Reighard). We can decide to settle for less than God's best for our lives.

— Sid Callaway —

6. Ask God for help. When we do this, God will give us peace.

I just made a decision that affected other lives. Two months ago, if asked, I would have never made the decision that I made. Then, without preparation or warning, I was faced with this decision. During prayer and listening to certain people, God gave me peace about His will, even though it would be unpopular to some. He not only guided me to make the right decision; he changed hearts as well.

We do not get to decide how long we will live, so we must make the best of all our decisions.

Pursuit:

1. What life-affecting decisions are you facing today? Home or work?

2. Are you settling, or are you listening to God for what His best is for you?

3. Are you allowing what others think of you to control what decisions you make?

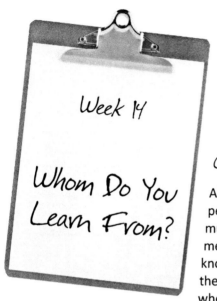

Week 14

Whom Do You Learn From?

Game Plan:
Jeremiah 1:5

Challenge:

All leaders learn from other people. Coaches learn so much from their peers and mentors and usually put this knowledge into practice in their coaching. This is evident when assistant coaches become head coaches because they take things from those they have worked with and for into their new position. This is true in any field.

I try to learn from everyone—teenagers, mentors, peers, and those I hold in high esteem. However, we must realize that even though we learn from many and use the principles of others (and this is a good thing), we cannot totally copy them or take their style completely into our situation.

Every situation is different to some degree, every team is a little different, but most of all, we are all different. God has given each of us unique gifts and abilities. That is why we cannot coach, lead, and teach just like someone else.

You are special. Jeremiah 1:5 says, "Before I formed you in the womb I knew you." Psalms 139:14 says, "I will give thanks to You, for I am fearfully and wonderfully made..." You are special with special gifts and talents. Use them for the glory of God. Do not believe Satan's lies for a single second. He wants us to think:

— Sid Callaway —

1. We have to win to be okay.
2. Others are better (for whatever reason) than we are.
3. We are no good.
4. We do not have ability.

These are all lies. You are special, you are a blessing, and you are a winner if you are on God's team. You can make a difference!

Pursuit:

1. Are you accepting who God made you to be, or are you trying to be just like someone else?

2. Claim Psalms 139:14 for yourself. Do not buy Satan's lies

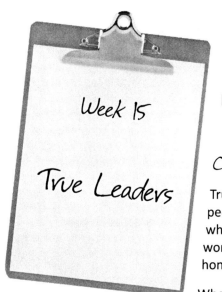

Week 15

True Leaders

Game Plan:
Matthew 5:16

Challenge:

True leaders are the ones people follow; they are those who can be trusted. In other words, leaders are people of honor, integrity, and character.

When I think of honor, I think of someone doing the right thing no matter what. No matter what others think, no matter who knows or does not know about the situation, no matter how difficult the task may be, and no matter how much he or she wants to bail out. Honor is never giving up on what you know is right.

Integrity is always being trustworthy. If people do not trust you, they will not follow you. I will not, anyway. I equate this to a military commander whose troops will gladly obey any order he gives, even in the fiercest of battles, regardless of their own thoughts or opinions. To have this following, they must totally trust him. Our teams must know we are honest and that we care for them, even above our own selves.

We have all heard that character is doing the right thing even if no one is looking. Scott Pilkington said, "You can't control what others say about you, but character is who you are regardless of what others say."

When you, as a leader, put these traits in practice in your life and totally trust and obey God's direction for your life,

— Sid Callaway —

you will be a leader worth following. Develop the heart of a champion as found in Mark 12:30: "Love the Lord your God with all your heart, soul and mind and strength."

Pursuit:

1. Are you a man or woman of honor, integrity, and character?

2. Do you totally trust God for His direction in your life?

— *Leadership Lessons for Coaches* —

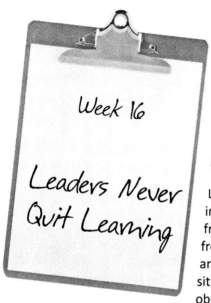

Week 16

Leaders Never Quit Learning

Game Plan:
Luke 15:11–24

Challenge:

Leaders must keep learning. It is important to learn from many sources. I learn from people my age, older, and younger. I also learn from situations, hardships, books, observations, and so forth.

One of the best sources to learn from is God's Word. He wrote His Game Plan for our lives for us to be successful. Once we have become a member of His team by repenting of our sins, asking forgiveness for our sins, accepting Christ's death on the cross as payment for our sins, and totally committing our lives to Him, we can have knowledge of the Word of God.

For example, here is what I learned after meditating on the story of the prodigal son found in Luke 15:

1. We all have a choice. We can choose to be winners, or we can choose to be losers.

2. We cannot be holy without discipline.

3. We must form good habits. There can be no exceptions for bad habits.

4. No one will help a sinking ship. Anyone can end up in the pigpen—those with good starts, those with bad starts.

5. We must repent of the sin in our lives to be saved and to be in the right relationship with God (if we are already saved).

6. None of us is worthy; it is by grace.

7. Notice who ran to whom! When we turn from sin, God runs to us.

8. Forgiveness is the best feeling in the world.

9. People are worth it.

10. Jealousy leads to bitterness. Bitterness destroys.

11. It is always better to stay the course.

12. We must grow daily—accountability, Bible study, prayer, church, desire, and passion.

13. Celebrate victories.

Pursuit:

Are you learning from God's Game Plan daily? If not, start today.

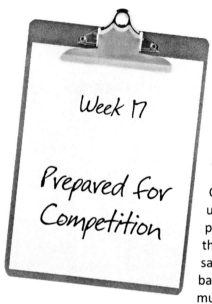

Week 17

Prepared for Competition

Game Plan:
Luke 15:11–24

Challenge:

Coaches, more so than most, understand about being prepared for competition. Along that line of thought, it is necessary that we understand that a battle is going on, and that we must be prepared.

Satan is out there trying to take us down. According to John Eldridge in his book, Wild at Heart, the first line of temptation Satan uses is that he tries to get us thinking that there is no battle. You cannot fight a battle you do not think exists (1 Peter 5:8–9).

If that does not work, he steps up the attack with intimidation and fear. When we fear our opponents, they have the upper hand. However, if we walk with Christ, we haven't a thing to fear.

If Satan cannot get to us with the above, he tries to get us to cut a deal with him. This is where he uses boredom, burnout, and complacency to get us to step over into sin. Remember, David stopped being a warrior and sent others to do his fighting for him (2 Sam. 11:1). If he had been fighting, he would not have noticed Bathsheba.

We do have a cause to fight for, and we, as leaders, must keep on fighting. Gideon, in the book of Judges, Chapter 7, had his army whittled down to three hundred. He got rid of the scared and incompetent, and he went to battle with the right team.

Victory will come to those who prepare, walk with Christ, and surround themselves with the right team but remember, not without a fight.

Pursuit:

1. What is your battle?

2. Are you complaining or fighting?

3. Who is on your team?

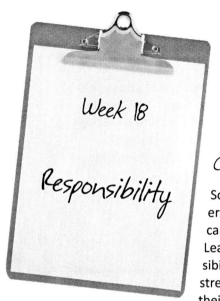

Week 18

Responsibility

Game Plan:
Luke 15:11–24

Challenge:

Someone once said that leaders must bear the burden or carry the load of their team. Leaders have great responsibility and so must have the strength and power to carry out their mission.

Some get their strength from others, but people still fail you at some point, even if they do not mean to. Some get their strength from themselves and their own abilities, but our own abilities cannot sustain us over time. Others get their strength from knowledge they gain, but knowledge can only take us so far.

To be the most effective, we must recognize that God is all-powerful, and we must let Him be the source of our strength. His Word is Truth, and it will never fail us.

Consider the following:

1. Psalm 27:1: "The Lord is my light and my salvation; whom shall I fear? The Lord is my strength of my life; of whom shall I be afraid?"

2. Psalm 29:11: "The Lord will give strength to His people...."

3. Psalm 46:1: "God is our refuge and strength, a very present help in trouble."

— Sid Callaway —

4. Proverbs 10:29: "The way of the Lord is strength for the upright, but destruction will come to the workers of iniquity."

5. Isaiah 40:29–31: "He gives power to the weak, and to those who have no might He increases strength, even youths shall faint and be weary, and the young men shall utterly fall, but those who wait on the Lord shall renew their strength...."

6. Zechariah 4:6: "...Not by might nor by power, but by my spirit, says the Lord of hosts."

Pursuit:

Where are you getting your strength?

— Leadership Lessons for Coaches —

Week 19

Insight

Game Plan:
Philippians 3:13–14

Challenge:

We often reflect on the past to gain insight about what our future goals should be. For example, it is helpful to think about our failures so hopefully we do not make the same mistakes again. It is good to remember successes and give thanks that God blessed us in such a way. It is also good to think about our relationships—both good and bad—and how God uses all things to work together for the good of His children. (See Romans 8:28.)

In thinking about the past, I have learned or, better said, "I am learning" several things:

1. We cannot live in the past. With some, "the older they get, the better they were."

2. Past hurts and problems need to be dealt with. If you leave them alone, they will creep up from time to time and cause problems.

3. Realize that we cannot change the past.

4. If we have wronged someone, try to work it out, ask forgiveness, or make restitution if necessary.

5. "Leave the irreparable past in God's hands and step out into the Irresistible future with Him" (Oswald Chambers).

— Sid Callaway —

6. Clebe McClary, a coach who joined the Marines and fought in Vietnam, uses the acronym FIDO (forget it and drive on).

7. Never lose hope; hope comes from God!

Pursuit:

1. Are you living in the past victories and failures? Are they driving your life?

2. What do you need to give over to God and "drive on"?

3. Where is your hope coming from?

Week 20

Achieve

Game Plan:
Luke 2:52

Challenge:

It is easy to look at leaders and say, "I'd sure like to be in their position." It is also easy, as leaders, to look at leaders of higher levels and say, "I'd sure like to be in their position." This can be a good thing. Most leaders want to achieve; that is why they are leaders.

In dealing with these aspirations, we must also understand something important. Usually, the higher we go, the more stress we have on us. All have pain and stress. All leaders have pain and stress to a higher degree. I love the quote in the movie, Spiderman, "With great power, comes great responsibility." With all the stress, responsibility, and the pain of life, we must still lead, inspire, motivate, and carry the load.

We all go through family problems, financial issues, loss of a friend or family member, critical decisions, and much more.

Here are a few suggestions:

- ✓ Pray much more! Learn to depend totally on God.

- ✓ Read promises in the Bible that God has made to His children.

- ✓ Pray against strongholds and attacks from the

enemy. Satan loves to try to get us when we are down. Remember, the name of Jesus and His blood shed for us is much more powerful than Satan could ever be.

✓ Seek out Godly mentors through personal contacts, books, and other media.

✓ Eat right, sleep right, and get enough exercise.

✓ Make sure you have one or two people that you can talk to about anything.

✓ Focus on the majors.

✓ Write down your thoughts.

✓ Give yourself a break.

✓ Do something fun. Even in grieving, it is ok to take a break. Remember, grieving has several stages, and they come and go, come again and go again, for various lengths of time.

✓ Minister to others.

Pursuit:

1. What are you trying to achieve? Is God the head of that plan?

2. Are you protecting yourself from physical, mental, and spiritual attack?

3. Are you so focused on your own issues that you have missed being a servant to someone else?

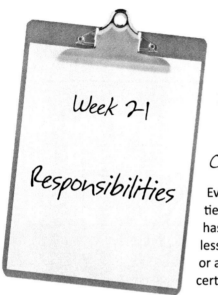

Week 21

Responsibilities

Challenge:

Every leader has responsibilities. Every person on the staff has responsibilities. Regardless, if you are the head coach or an assistant coach, you have certain responsibilities.

The best-case scenario is that there are leaders at all levels. We have all heard the phrase, "Too many chiefs and not enough Indians." However, true leaders work just like the rest of the staff. Also, the more leader types you have within the organization, the better the team is.

So, everyone in a position of leadership has the responsibility of improving himself or herself in several areas. For example:

1. People skills. This is a high priority, as leaders deal with people.
2. Organization. We can improve, even if we are not good in this area.
3. Planning.
4. Communication.
5. Listening.
6. Handling conflict.
7. Vision.
8. Recognizing weaknesses.

— Sid Callaway —

9. Depending on God. This is the main one.

Pursuit:

1. What areas do you need to improve in?

2. Set goals and reasonable ways to reach them.

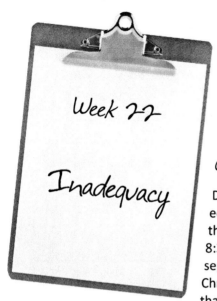

Week 22

Inadequacy

Game Plan:
Romans 8:35–39

Challenge:

Do leaders ever feel inadequate? Absolutely! Even though we learn in Romans 8:35–39 that "nothing can separate us from the love of Christ" and that we are "more than conquerors through Christ," we sometimes feel inadequate. We question our actions and feel insecure.

A few weeks ago, I was struggling with a decision I had made. I had prayed, talked to the people in charge, reasoned, and searched, but I still felt horrible. So, I called my accountability partner and told him that I had so much happening that I was questioning my every move. He immediately affirmed the decision I had made. It, along with hearing some good teaching on feelings of inadequacy, made me realize that leaders are not always confident and are subject to doubts and feeling inferior and inadequate just like everyone else.

Romans 7:21–24 says, "I find then a law, that evil is present with me, the one who wills to do good. For I delight in the law of God according to the inward man. But I see another law in my members, warring against the law of my mind, and bringing me into captivity to the law of sin which is my members. O wretched man that I am! Who will deliver me from this body of death?" Paul offers this, not as an excuse, but as a fact.

— Sid Callaway —

We definitely struggle—sometimes a lot, sometimes not so much. According to Dr. Stanley, we must realize the following:

1. Some feelings of inadequacy are legitimate. We are not good at everything.

2. We can be defeated by it or learn from it.

3. We must let inadequacy drive us to God.

4. We can be relieved of the burden of living on our own strength.

Pursuit:

1. Are you letting your inadequacies tear you down, or are you learning from them?

2. Have you let go and let God carry your burdens?

3. Are you standing on His promises?

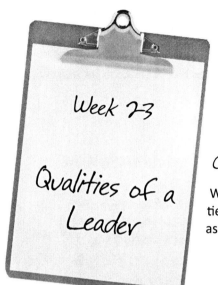

Week 23

Qualities of a Leader

Game Plan:
Romans 12:3–8

Challenge:

We always hear about qualities of a leader—qualities such as the following:

✓ Communication skills

✓ Integrity

✓ Focus

✓ Influence

✓ Charisma

✓ Relationships

✓ Vision

✓ Dependability

✓ Encouragement

We often read lists, see certain qualities in others, and begin to think we just were left out. The truth is that God has given us all gifts and abilities. Another truth is that no one is good at everything. One more truth is that all of us have special

— Sid Callaway —

and unique gifts, which God gave us so that we could use them to benefit the team—His team, the body of Christ.

We may have gifts that we do not hear about too often, such as the following:

1. *Compassion*. Caring and checking on friends, teammates, and others.

2. *Reading moods*. This can help us in ministering to the needs of others.

3. *Saving*. Saving money for the future need—personal or for someone else. Also, saving yourself from personal burnout and self-destruction.

4. *Knowledge*. A special sense of knowing what is about to happen or what could happen. We must be careful that we are totally in line with God if we have and use this gift.

5. *Patience*.

6. *Confrontation*. To confront someone about a problem is tough. Some have a special gift to do it tactfully.

7. *Timing*. Being on time—being able to manage time in travel, events, and schedules.

Pursuit:

1. What are you gifted in?

2. Are you using your gifts for the team, or are you using them against the team?

3. Is your pride about your gifts getting in the way of your witness?

Week 24

Rebuilding

**Game Plan:
Nehemiah 2:5**

Challenge:

There are times when all leaders have to regroup, start over, or rebuild. I have thought of several things that must happen for this to happen successfully.

✓ Evaluate the past—what got you there

- Failures
- Successes
- Personnel
- Techniques

✓ Check your passion. Is this where you are supposed to be?

✓ Move from the past to the present

✓ Where are you right now?

- Current strengths
- Current weaknesses
- Returning players
- New players

✓ Ask the question—what will it take to achieve your goals?
- Staff
- Money
- Time
- Who can help

✓ Seek God's Guidance
- Obey

Pursuit:

1. What is your passion about? Is it God centered?

2. Set goals and actively pursue the task.

3. Have you first sought out God's wisdom on it all?

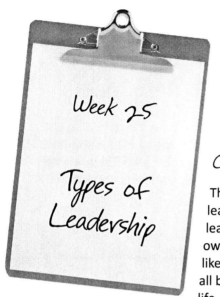

Week 25

Types of
Leadership

**Game Plan:
1 Corinthians 12:4–6**

Challenge:

There are many styles of
leadership. This is because all
leaders are different, with their
own gifts, personalities, bents,
likes, and dislikes. Also, we have
all been down different roads in
life. All this comes into play.

All good types of leadership can be effective. I guess the best
leaders display many types of leadership depending on the
situation. Some good types of effective leadership are

The Humble Leader
It is hard to follow someone who is cocky, arrogant, and
knows everything. King Solomon asked God for wisdom when
he could have asked for anything. Leaders need to admit
their weaknesses and mistakes. After all, their people know
them anyway, and it will let them see true humility.

The Compassionate Leader
Jesus could have blasted the woman caught in adultery. He
did not excuse her sin, but he did show compassion. I have
learned over the years to give grace and mercy to people
because I need these things from God.

The Goal-Oriented Leader
Everything this leader does has a purpose in mind, and it is
for the best interest of the team and the person.

— Sid Callaway —

The Servant-Leader
This leader serves his team. He is there for them often helping them achieve their dreams and goals. This leader has the best interest of others in mind.

The Courageous Leader
This leader will take a stand for the team, for principles, and for people. They are not unduly concerned with what others think, but are focused on doing what is right if there is a big price to pay. The Apostle Paul never backed down when he knew he was right.

Pursuit:

1. What kind of leader are you?

2. Are you raising up leaders around you?

3. Are you leading for the benefit of the team or for your own self?

Week 26

Authority

Game Plan:
Matthew 20:28

Challenge:

Leaders have authority for
several reasons:

1. They have earned the position of authority.
2. They have been around for a long time.
3. They have most of the knowledge.

Leaders are definitely the most effective when they see
themselves as part of the team, leading by example. When
a leader understands that, he or she does not have to know
more, be more skilled, or have more experience. He or she
can then be freed up to lead by serving and by example.
Leaders can have people on their team who are better in
certain areas than they are— the means by which true leadership takes place.

When leaders serve their staff, take care of them, help them,
stand by them, and fight for them, then the leaders have
earned their positions of leadership. This is when they have
influence and authority. Others will be glad to follow them at
this point.

Remember, leaders are not a one-person show!

— Sid Callaway —

Pursuit:

1. Are you serving in your area of leadership?

2. Are you standing by your team and leading them toward a main goal? Or are they all running around doing their own thing, not being aware of the main goal?

3. Are you trying to be a one-person show?

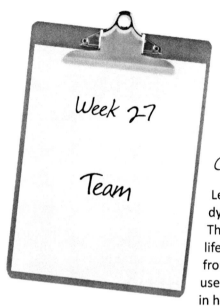

Week 27

Team

Game Plan:
1 Corinthians 9:24

Challenge:

Leadership is so much like the dynamics of an athletic team. There are many leadership and life principles that can be taken from sports. The Apostle Paul uses much athletic terminology in his epistles. In 1 Corinthians 9:24, he says "Do you not know that those who run in a race all run, but one receives the prize? Run in such a way that you may obtain it."

Some examples of leadership comparisons are the following:

✓ A great team not only needs a head coach, but also other coaches as well. Even though the head coach is the main leader, the team is much better off if the assistant coaches are leaders also. Leadership at all levels works best.

✓ Every team needs a game plan. Every coach needs to be organized and to have a plan of action for every game, depending on the opponents and their strengths and weaknesses. Leadership is all about strategizing and organizing.

✓ Teams must practice. When we are prepared,

   • Obstacles do not take us out.

- We play with confidence.
- We have fun.

✓ Great teams work hard, smart, and are consistent and disciplined. They achieve their accomplishments. Leaders must set the example of discipline, consistency, and hard work.

✓ The members of a team must support one another and be unselfish if great things are to be achieved. Leaders must be unselfish and must sacrifice for the good of those they lead.

✓ A great team must focus on winning and doing everything it takes to win. Leaders must focus on success—not past or possible failures.

✓ A great team is prepared. Leaders prepare themselves and those they lead.

✓ Teams that win have a great attitude. Leaders go through tough times but must keep displaying a good attitude.

✓ Teams that win listen to their coaches. All leaders must also be followers. Leaders seek people, principles, and examples to follow.

✓ Teams that emphasize the basics seem to play to a higher standard.

✓ Leaders who do the small things—writing notes, returning calls, encouraging, and serving—gain influence.

Pursuit:

1. Are you working with discipline and consistency?

2. Is your team supporting one another?

3. Are you doing the "small" things?

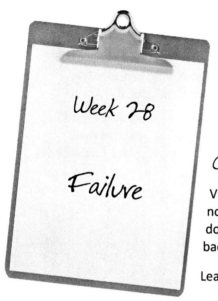

Week 28

Failure

Game Plan:
Luke 22:54–62

Challenge:

Vince Lombardi said, "It's not whether you get knocked down; it's whether you get back up that counts."

Leaders sometimes *fail*.

It is not about if we fail or not. It is all about what we do after we fail that counts. Max Lucado said, "Failure is not final." John Maxwell says we must learn to "fail forward." Great dreams and ideas go untested because we are afraid of failure.

Some further thoughts on this subject:

✓ Remember we are all in the same boat. Whether we want to admit it or not, we are all human with limitations.

✓ A great way to make fewer mistakes is to surround yourself with people better than you are. That is a thought worth considering.

✓ Plan. It was not raining when Noah built the Ark.

✓ Someone once said, "I'm 40 years old, I am too old to go back to school. I will be 44 years old when I finish." Guess what? In 4 years, you will be 44 years old anyway!

— Sid Callaway —

✓ Remember this: Amateurs built the ark; professionals built the Titanic.

✓ Do not worry so much about what others think. If they are human, they have failed also.

If we are on team Jesus Christ, we are on the winning team. We still have to play the game; we still get our share of bumps and bruises. However, we must keep our focus on the victory—victory that counts.

Pursuit:

1. Are your failures knocking you down, or are you using them as stepping stones?

2. What is your plan B?

3. Are you living under God's standard or man's? This strongly decides your perspective of failure and success.

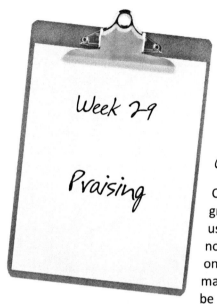

Week 29

Praising

Game Plan:
Hebrews 3:13

Challenge:

Coach John Wooden, the great UCLA basketball coach, used to tell his players to wink, nod, or give a high five or a pat on the back to the player who made it possible for the shot to be made. A player once asked him, "Coach, what if in the heat of the game, they don't look?" Coach Wooden said, "They'll always look."

We all need encouragement. Some of the players you coach do not get too much of that at home. You are the only positive role model in many players' lives. In other words, you have the ability to make or break a young person. That is a heavy responsibility. In light of that, I hope you will purpose to be a great encourager.

An encourager:

1. Praises in public, criticizes in private.
2. Says five times more positive things than negative things.
3. Cares about the total person, not just the athletic ability.
4. Is approachable and has time to talk and listen.
5. Makes others feel good about themselves.

— Sid Callaway —

When I was in college, a high school football player that looked up to me asked me to watch one of his practices. I soon found time to do so. As I watched, my young friend was being knocked around, missed tackles, and he just looked terrible. After practice, I asked him what he thought of his teammates. His response was "They are all so much better than me." I immediately told him that he was the strongest and toughest guy on the team. A few weeks later, I was able to attend another practice. Everyone was afraid of him.

Encouragement—it is great to get and better to give!

Pursuit:

1. Are you praising your team or criticizing your team most?

2. Are you taking time to listen to your teammates and encourage them where they might be feeling like a failure?

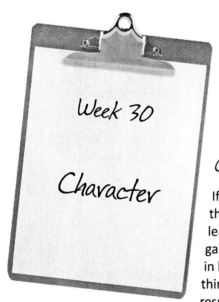

Week 30

Character

**Game Plan:
Matthew 5:37**

Challenge:

If a leader moves beyond the positional level of leadership, he or she must gain the respect of those in his or her influence. One thing we must do is gain respect of those we lead.

According to John Maxwell, respect affects leadership in the following ways:

1. When a leader gains respect, then leading becomes easier.

2. Respect is a matter of leadership, not position, title, or gender.

3. Respect is the highest level of leadership.

4. The highest compliment to a leader—other leaders follow.

In thinking about these statements, may I suggest several ways in which one gains respect:

✓ *Giving respect*. A principle goes like this: You give what you need. If you need love, give love. If you need respect, then give respect to those you lead.

✓ *Being dependable*. Everyone wants to follow a leader that he or she can depend on. Try this:

Make it a rule to return your phone calls within 24 hours, or have someone do it for you if you are unavailable.

✓ *Keeping your word.* If you tell someone you are going to do something, do it.

✓ *Helping others reach potential.* Do not just help people for your sake. Help them for their sake.

Pursuit:

1. Do you do what you say you are going to do?

2. Are you on time?

3. What do others say about your integrity and character?

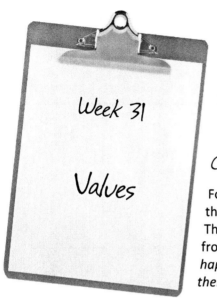

Week 31

Values

Game Plan:
Exodus 14:13

Challenge:

For a team to be united, the team must have values. These values must come from the coach. *For this to happen, coaches must value their players.*

Ways to show value to your team:

✓ *Hold a team together.* A few years ago when Tylenol had a big scare, the president of the company pulled their product from the stores. This decision cost them 100 million dollars. When asked how he made that decision so quickly, he said, "It's easy to do the right thing when you know ahead of time where you stand."

✓ *Give stability.* It is important to be worthy of your team's trust and respect.

✓ *Set standards for performance.* The great Coach Landry said, "Coaching is simply getting people to do what they don't want to do to achieve what they want to achieve."

✓ *Guide and give direction.* Who you are speaks louder than what you say.

— Sid Callaway —

✓ *Attract like-minded people.* You attract who you are (John Maxwell).

Pursuit:

1. Have you ever valued your team?

2. If so, how did they react?

Week 32

Improvement

Game Plan:
Philippians 2:15 says we are to have the attitude of Jesus Christ. If we do, our leadership skills will go up several notches.

Challenge:

Some people are more gifted in leadership than others are. However, everyone can improve his or her leadership abilities. So, those of us in leadership positions must constantly work on our skills.

One leadership quality that great leaders have is the ability to value everyone on their team. In other words, great leaders can recognize the gifts and skills of a team member and use them for the benefit of the team and team member as well. This encourages the team member and makes him feel like a major part of the team. I love the quote by Lou Holtz: "I praise loudly and criticize softly."

The best leader of all time is Jesus Christ. Consider a few examples:

✓ Jesus had great compassion for those on His team (John 11:32–35).

✓ Jesus served those on His team (John 13:5).

✓ Jesus comforted those on His team (John 14:1–6).

✓ Jesus gave commands to those on His team (John 15:17).

✓ Jesus prayed for those on His team (John 17:13–26).

✓ Jesus confirmed those on His team when they made a mistake (Matt. 26:69–75/John 21:15–17).

Pursuit:

1. Do I show that I value my team? If so, how? If not, plan to do so.

2. Do I find myself criticizing more than praising?

3. Identify someone on your team that you need to invest time in.

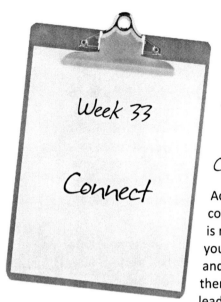

Week 33

Connect

**Game Plan:
John 13:3–5**

Challenge:

According to John Maxwell, connecting with your people is not an option as a leader. If you do not take time, effort, and energy to connect with them, you will not be able to lead them effectively.

So, how do you connect? Here are a few suggestions:

✓ *Be an encourager.* Continually build up, never down. A coach who personally attacks, embarrasses, and curses a player is not building the player up.

✓ *Teach your sport in a way the players can learn.* The "It's my way or the highway" mentality is usually fatal. Be open to new ideas and new research.

✓ *Make sure the team is ready.* Readiness builds confidence. They must be in proper condition but not overtrained. They also must know the playbook.

✓ *Realize it is okay to have fun.* I read where one day after practice, a football coach told the team that if the kicker made a field goal from a certain distance that there would be no sprints that day.

— *Sid Callaway* —

He did make it, and morale was boosted. An occasional cookout or completely different type of practice is good for the team and coaches alike.

✓ *Make each player feel important by giving him or her a job on the team.* Surely, not everyone can be a starter, but everyone can contribute. Giving a player a permanent spot on special teams in football, or the job of running in plays, or giving a starter one play or five-minute rest can make all the difference in how a kid views himself or herself.

✓ *A good leader always puts his/her team first.* Are your players more important than the final score?

Because Jesus Christ gave His life to connect with us, I think the "law of connection" is worth giving some thought. Remember, coach, the most important thing you can do for your team is make sure you are on the team—Team Jesus Christ.

Pursuit:

1. Have I been putting my players first over the final score?

2. Is there a team member that needs my support and encouragement? If so, plan and pin time to work with that player.

3. Am I teaching my players on a level they can understand?

Week 34

Daddy

Game Plan:
Psalms 68:5

Challenge:

A coach once made the comment to FCA's earlier president, Dal Shealy, that he was the daddy to all his players. That is a frightening thought. Coaches on all levels play an important role in the lives of their teams, including as substitute parents. It means that you are not just developing athletes but lives as well—lives that will end up in destruction or lives that will make a difference.

As a parent, I naturally want the best for my son. I pray that God will develop him athletically, that God will build him mentally, that he will be blessed with a great wife one day, have great friends, and have a wonderful job. But, most of all, I pray that my son will walk with God. If you are a parent, I hope you wish the same thing for your children.

If you are a substitute parent or even a role model for a player who has great parents, what do you want the most for your players? Your answer to this will tell you much about your own relationship with God. I hope each of you is on God's team. However, it is possible that several of you are not.

God loves us so much and because He knew that we are not good enough to make His team, He made the team for us through Jesus Christ (God in the flesh). Our good works will never earn us a spot on God's team. We must accept what

Christ did for us—taking our sin on Himself and dying for our sins. We must ask Him to forgive us and we must turn from our sin. We must also commit to Him and follow His Game Plan—the Bible.

If you are struggling with whether you are on God's team, remember this: If you are on His team, you will have a great desire for God and the things you do will result from that desire.

Isaiah 59:2	1 Corinthians 15:3–6
Romans 6:23	2 Corinthians 14:6
Hebrews 9:27	John 1:12–13
Isaiah 64:6	Romans 10:9, 10, 13

Pursuit:

1. Who is on your team? Are you taking your job seriously and reaching into your players to grow up as strong people—mentally, spiritually, and physically?

2. Who is your coach? Are you a disciplined athlete on His team, strengthening your walk with Him daily?

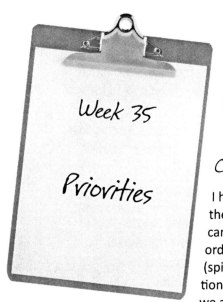

Week 35

Priorities

Game Plan:
Matthew 6:33

Challenge:

I have discovered that one of the most important things we can do is get our priorities in order. We all have three areas (spiritual, physical, and emotional) that must be in check if we are to function at our best.

For example, it is possible to be growing spiritually in your relationship with God and to be in great physical condition and yet be depleted emotionally. If we become out of balance, we can expect certain problems, and these problems will keep us from being our best. I have always said that we must eat, sleep, and exercise right to feel good. We must keep in mind that there are even more important things than feeling good.

Our no. 1 priority is not debatable; it is our relationship with God (see Matthew 6:33). I completely believe that our families are no. 2.

Mike Nappa, author of The Courage to be a Christian outlines ten principles for proper prioritizing. They are the following:

1. Always remember God is first—no matter what. Actually, God wants to be 100% of every area of our lives.

2. Invest in your family, and you will earn "joy interest" for the rest of your life.

3. You reap what you sow. Let your actions and attitudes today sow seeds you will be glad to harvest tomorrow.

4. Before making a decision, ask, "Which of my life priorities does this conflict with? Which is the greater priority?"

5. Be aware of your physical, emotional, spiritual, and relational resources and know their limits. Use your resources to the limit, but do not go beyond them until God extends the limit.

6. It is better to say no right now than to say I am sorry later.

7. When it comes to opportunities, not every open door is one you should walk through. Wait until you see God on the other side before you take that step of faith.

8. When you say yes, let your actions and attitudes confirm your promise.

9. Satan is a liar. Do not believe his promises.

10. Every minute of your life counts. Live in such a way that each of your minutes says yes to God's will.

Pursuit:

1. List your priorities. Be honest. (Where is God on your list?)

2. Are you taking time to take care of your physical body? If not, make a plan, and stick to it.

3. Are you lined up with Christ to hear what He has called you to do? Are you ready to armor up and to go to battle?

— Sid Callaway —

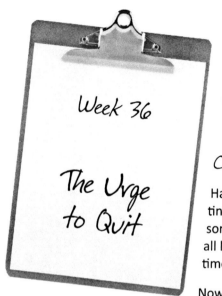

Week 36

The Urge
to Quit

Game Plan:
Hebrews 12:1–3

Challenge:

Have you ever felt like quitting? You probably have at some time or another. I believe all leaders get discouraged at times.

Now, I am not talking about changing directions because of God's leading or for family or personal reasons. I remember when Coach Bill McCartney left coaching to start Promise Keepers. Sometimes, God leads us in other directions and we have to be obedient. However, if you are on the verge of just quitting, please consider the following:

✓ Who cares for me?

✓ You may think the whole world is against you, but I bet if the truth were known, many people love you and will stick with you.

✓ Whom do I care about?

✓ I remember staying in a bad situation a long time because of my love for people under my authority.

✓ Have I kept myself "sharp"? We might think that we do not have the time, but we do have the time to stay sharp. The lumberjack who took time to

— Sid Callaway —

sharpen his ax got behind at first but more than made up the difference later.

- ✓ People are people.
- ✓ The grass is usually not "greener on the other side."
- ✓ There is no perfect place.
- ✓ Am I taking time to recharge?
- ✓ We all have three gauges: spiritual, physical, and emotional. If one or more of these is out of balance for a long time, we are headed for disaster.

Pursuit:

1. What has caused me to get to the state where I want to quit?

2. Do I have my accountability in place?

3. Am I letting every situation drive me closer to God?

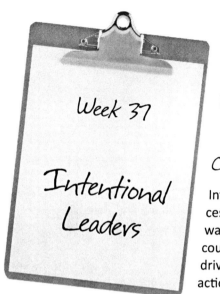

Week 37

Intentional
Leaders

Game Plan:
Matthew 5, 6, and 7

Challenge:

Intentional leaders are successful leaders who have a
way of making every move
count. They are purpose
driven, they maintain a plan of
action, and they are organized.

Intentional leaders:

1. *Care*. They let their staff and co-workers know
   that they are valued. They check on them and get
   involved in their personal lives. This lets others
   know that they are important.

2. *Applaud*. They give credit where credit is due. I
   heard that Coach Bear Bryant said, "When anything goes great, they did it. When anything goes
   semi-great, we did it. When anything goes bad, I
   did it."

3. *Encourage*. They encourage all those around
   them. A man named Henry H. Goddard invented
   a machine that measures fatigue. Tests revealed
   that when subjects were spoken to with positive
   words of encouragement, energy went up, but
   when spoken to in a discouraging way, energy
   went down.

— Sid Callaway —

4. *Give attention to the insignificant.* They do the little things. The little things are usually the things no one, at least not many, see you do. God sees, and this is where character is built.

Pursuit:

1. Have I cared for others around me and their life situations more than I have cared about my own personal needs?

2. Have I applauded and encouraged others around me on a regular basis?

3. Am I acknowledging people around me that go the extra mile and do the little things?

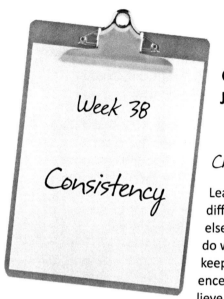

Week 38

Consistency

Game Plan:
Joshua 1:1–2

Challenge:

Leaders go through tough and difficult times just as everyone else does. The question is how do we continue to do our job, keep our focus, make a difference, and reach our goals? I believe the answer is consistency.

In Joshua 1:1–2, God ordained Joshua to take over after the death of Moses. Why? Consistency.

- ✓ Joshua and Caleb gave a true and bold report when they were spying on the land of Canaan.

- ✓ Joshua faithfully served under Moses for all those years.

- ✓ Joshua lived a life of obedience.

When good times are good and when bad times are bad, keep on doing what you are called to do. Keep having your quiet time, keep going to church, exercising, spending time with your family, and so forth. There may be an initial time of being out of sync but get back to your consistent lifestyle.

The runners lined up ready to go
All sizes and shapes, from fast to slow.
They came from various cities, towns, and states.
To compete—they'd trained for this date.

While all were serious, their techniques varied quite a bit.
They had different plans to make themselves a hit.
Some sprinted off the starting line while others set a pace.
Everyone had different strategies of how they'd win the race.

As the race went on some grew tired way to quick.
Others went way to slow, even for a final kick.
But, out of nowhere came a winner everyone could see.
He told the interviewer, his secret was consistency.

                                            —Unknown

"Consistency will make good athletes great, get you through the times you hate, 'cause you pay the price and is a sure thing, not just a throw of a dice"

Pursuit:

1. Have I been consistent with my prayer and quiet time?

2. Am I being obedient to do the things God asks me to do with boldness and truth?

3. Am I letting situations control me, or am I letting God control the situations?

Week 39

Future

Game Plan:
Deuteronomy 30:15–20

Challenge:

I believe all leaders must spend some time thinking, reflecting, and making choices about the future. All this must be done before the Lord so that He can guide us properly.

On New Year's Day one year, I did some of this that resulted in a list of several choices I had made, which will hopefully dictate the way I live my life, lead my family, do my job, and honor my Lord.

Not that I am going to share my whole list, but my first choice is life. Along with that go many things because if we choose life, we must choose to live totally for the One who gives life. This is where it all begins.

I sincerely hope and pray that every choice you make will come from your relationship with Jesus Christ. To have this relationship, you must choose to accept Him and that He paid the price for our sins. It is all about what He has done for us, not what we can do for Him. Make his Word your guide for everything, and let's pray for one another that we will "go the distance" and be "strong to the finish."

— Sid Callaway —

Pursuit:

1. How is my relationship with Christ?

2. Am I living totally for Him?

3. Am I seeking God's plan for my future?

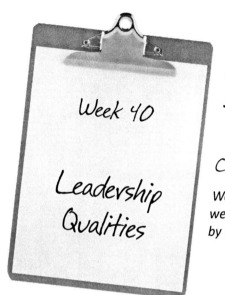

Week 40

Leadership
Qualities

**Game Plan:
John 15:13**

Challenge:

*We make a living by what
we get, but we make a life
by what we give.*

—Sir Winston Churchill

Leaders are givers.

Leaders make a difference by pouring themselves into the lives of those they lead and influence.

Leaders do far more than what is visible to the public.

Leaders do not only deal with the problems and pressures of their positions, but also of those under their leadership.

Leaders are a part of the team and share in the responsibilities.

Leaders are real. Anyone can blow smoke.

Leaders are fighters; they fight for the cause and for others.

Being a leader costs much. Not all are willing to pay the price.

Pursuit:

1. Am I willing to pay the price for my team?

2. Am I being real, or am I putting on a mask for my team?

3. Am I giving of myself or taking for myself?

Week 41

A Good Name

Game Plan:
Proverbs 22:1

Challenge:

Good leaders are observant
and are constantly learning.
We can learn something from
almost everyone—people we
know, people we do not know,
friends, family, teammates,
work associates, pastors, teach-
ers, authors, older and younger people. Here are just a few
things I have learned from others. I will leave out names and
titles, so you can fill in your own. Many of these I am still
learning and have a long way to go.

From _____ I learned how to love.

From _____ I learned patience
and unselfishness.

From _____ I learned to get up
early and make the most of my day.

From _____ I learned to memo-
rize scripture.

From _____ I learned to have
daily quiet times.

From _____ I learned to under-
stand that everyone is different, and everyone should
be treated differently.

From _____ I learned to loosen
up and have fun.

From _____ I learned that we
must take care of ourselves physically, spiritually, and
emotionally.

From _____ I learned balance.

From _____ I learned that we
cannot expect everyone to be at the same level as we are.

From _____ I learned to concentrate on my strengths.

From _____ I learned that at-
titude is the difference maker in most situations.

From _____ I learned that God
can use anybody.

From _____ I learned that leaders are servants.

From _____ I learned that we
should go the distance for our team.

Pursuit:

1. Who are my audience, and what am I teaching them with my life?

2. Whom do I look to, and are they teaching God's ways or their ways?

3. What am I doing with what I have learned?

— Sid Callaway —

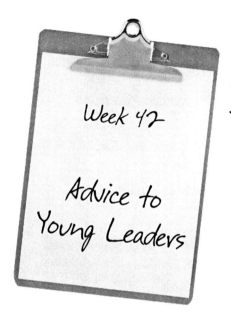

Week 42

Advice to
Young Leaders

Game Plan:
James 1:5

✓ Leading people is a privilege. If you are given such an opportunity, it will be profitable to you and to those you lead to be a good leader. Everyone has a choice about the type of leader he or she will become.

✓ Early on, decide what you would like said about you after you die, and start living that way now.

✓ Get in, and stay in, great physical condition.

✓ Maintain a balance. This will help keep you from depression and burnout.

✓ Make sure your family in is second to God alone, and that they are getting the time from you that they deserve. If not, resign some of your duties.

✓ Remember, you are living for those you lead. (This includes your family, those you are now leading, and those you will lead in the future.)

— Sid Callaway —

✓ As you get older and more experienced in life and in leading, narrow your focus to your strengths.

✓ Be sure to practice good financial principles, and stay out of debt.

✓ Develop the habit of spending time with God every day—throughout the day.

✓ Do some things that are out of your comfort zone.

Plan as if you will live forever and live as if this is your last day.
—Unknown

Pursuit:

1. Am I spending time every day with God?

2. Am I leading my family the way God would have me lead, or am I letting someone else lead them?

3. Do I have a balance in my life spiritually and physically?

Week 43

Keep Growing

Game Plan:
Luke 2:52

Challenge:

It is easy to stand still and even regress, but we must keep growing. Someone once said that when we stop growing, we die—maybe not physically, but in every other way. With all the high tech knowledge out there, coaches and athletes must keep up, or they will get behind in a hurry. So, I encourage you to grow and increase in all areas of your life.

Signs of a growing person:

1. reading the Bible and other good books
2. getting around people with more knowledge and experience than you
3. making plans to grow
4. getting out of your comfort zone
5. going after new goals—inside and outside your profession
6. studying successful people
7. listening to authority
8. having a good attitude and never being a know-it-all

— Sid Callaway —

Pursuit:

1. What areas of my life do I need to increase and grow?

2. What is my Game Plan?

3. What areas have I regressed in, and what am I going to do to ignite growth in those areas?

— Leadership Lessons for Coaches —

Week 44

Leadership
Requirements

Game Plan:
Galatians 5:22–23

Challenge:

Below are five important qualities for all leaders. There are many more, but unless we get these, we will always be lacking:

Serve
Leaders should serve. Leaders need to serve those they lead and others as well. I once saw Dan Cathy, president of Chick-fil-A, Inc., serving all the corporate office staff during lunch at their cafeteria. It is in serving, that we gain opportunities to lead, train, and have an impact on another life. Matthew 5:4 talks about going the second mile. The first mile is expected. So, on the second mile is where we have opportunities to influence and make a difference.

Give up
According to John Maxwell, you have to give up to go up. It costs to be a leader. Leaders usually work harder, carry more burdens, and sacrifice more than others sacrifice. Walter Payton was a great player and leader on the Chicago Bears football team but probably worked harder than most of the other players. They say his off-season workouts were killers.

Relationships
Leaders build relationships. It takes time and effort to build relationships with others. People must know that you care.

— Sid Callaway —

I once had a supervisor who spent time with me on and off duty, building a relationship with me. He was demanding, but I never minded following his orders because he cared. (In college, I had a coach who was hard on us. At first, I did not like him until I learned how much he cared. He spent much time and effort on me to the point where I would run through a wall if he told me to.)

Discipline
"It is your discipline, not your desire that determines your destiny" (Coach Frosty Westering). How many times have you heard people say, "I wish I could_____ as good as _____"? You can sit around and wish all day. At the end of the day, you are no better off than when you began. It takes action to go to another level.

People versus *plan leaders are not lone rangers*
Great leaders are always looking for others to inspire, encourage, and teach them. Leaders are always looking to build relationships because others are important. Remember, people are more important than the plan.

We are to serve others as Christ served. It is only with Him, through Him, and because of Him, that we can be what we should. We must continually build on our relationships with Him. He is our no. 1 relationship.

Pursuit:

1. Am I willing to sacrifice for the team?

2. How am I doing by building trust through relationships?

3. Am I training for discipline, or am I giving in?

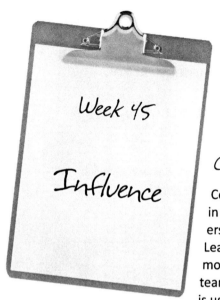

Week 45

Influence

Game Plan:
Colossians 3:23

Challenge:

Coaches have much influence in our society and are leaders because of their position. Leadership is influence. The most influential person on a team, in a business, and so forth is usually the leader. I think we can all gain more influence by working on certain skills.

1. *Be a leader with integrity.* Let your word be your word and be above reproach in all your dealings.

2. *Be an encourager.* Coaches can encourage or discourage. Coaches can build up or tear down. Examine your coaching style on a regular basis.

3. *Raise the level.* Enlarge those you coach. Take an interest in every aspect of your players, and generate an atmosphere of growth.

4. *Be accepting.* Accept each player for who they are. Do not let your acceptance be based on performance. If they know you care, they will work much harder.

Pursuit:

1. Am I consistently encouraging my team?

2. Am I showing concern for my team to help them grow or because I want the glory?

3. Good, bad, or somewhere in between, do I accept my teammates for who they are?

Week 46

Giving Your Best

Game Plan:
Colossians 3:23

Challenge:

Character is always lost when a high ideal is sacrificed on the altar of conformity and popularity.

—Chuck Swindoll

At a breakfast meeting with Coach Bobby Bowden of FSU, he said that his goal was to get all his players to play to the best of their ability. Coaches are leaders because of their position; you are positional leaders. However, you must move from being a positional leader quickly if you are to influence your players to play to the best of their ability.

According to John Maxwell, there are at least four more levels of leadership in addition to the positional leader:

✓ Permission level. Here, you are building relation-ships, and people follow you because they want to.

✓ Production level. People are now following you because of what you have done for the team. Problems at this level are fixed with little effort. Momentum is in place. You are producing wanted results.

✓ People development level. People are following you because of what you have done for them. You are, at this level, investing your life in the lives of your team. You care more for them as a person than as athletes. Coach Bowden further said that day that he shares the Gospel of Jesus Christ with all his players. They have a team devotion each week. He is actually preparing them for the whole spectrum of life.

✓ Personhood level. At this level, people follow you because they respect you. You are, at this level, a person of character and integrity. People want what you have.

You must commit to the high road, the narrow path, the second mile, if you are going to be a leader with the highest level of impact.

Pursuit:

1. What level am I on? Where do I need to be?

2. Do I have the respect of my team, or do they follow me because they have to?

3. Where do I stand on a "character" basis?

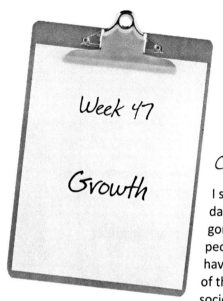

Week 47

Growth

Game Plan:
2 Peter 3:18

Challenge:

I spoke with a coach the other day who told me that he had gone into coaching to help people. If you are a coach, you have the potential to be one of the greatest ministers in our society. This is because:

1. You are in a special position of influence.
2. You have earned the right to be heard.
3. You have the potential to be a great (if not the only) positive role model for a young person.

Because of these things, you must do what all great leaders do—grow continuously.

Some old training methods are outdated, and there are new ways of doing things that work. Because of this, you must keep studying, learning, and growing, so you can pass the information on to your team, so they can reach their highest potential.

Most important is your need to keep growing in Christ by studying God's Word, having fellowship with other Christians, being accountable, participating in Church, and sharing your faith.

God's Game Plan is exciting, and it is important to know this plan and pass it along to your team and others. After all, which is more important—"your game" or "God's Game"?

Pursuit:

1. Am I growing in Christ or living in the past knowledge and experiences with Christ?

2. Whose game plan have I been putting first?

Week 48

Risktakers

Game Plan:
Philippians 4, 13

Challenge:

I am told that leaders can be put into one of three categories:

✓ *Caretakers.* The leader can maintain what the earlier leader built. Status quo is their purpose.

✓ *Undertakers.* The leader can kill what has been built or developed. This type of leader is lazy and not willing to pay the price.

✓ *Risktakers.* This leader takes calculated risks. They are "go getters" who are always trying to take their team to the next level. They are willing to stick out their necks. A good example of this is the New York Giants NFL head coach who said, "This team is going to the playoffs. I am putting MY neck on the line. I'm taking the responsibility."

The risktakers are the ones going somewhere. Do not hesitate to try something new. The old way may not work anymore. John Maxwell said, "If the horse is dead—dismount."

— *Sid Callaway* —

- ✓ David put it all on the line to fight Goliath.

- ✓ Walt Disney took a chance by drawing a mouse that ran across the floor and trying to sell the idea of Mickey Mouse.

- ✓ A preacher by the name of David Wilkerson took a risk and shared the Gospel to a young gang member named Nicky Cruise—results: He accepted Christ, and he has led many to a personal relationship with Jesus Christ.

- ✓ Wilma Rudolph's mother took a risk by telling her young crippled daughter that she could achieve any goal she wanted. Wilma Rudolph is remembered as one of America's greatest track athletes and an Olympic gold medalist.

Following Christ involves many risks. Remember this; they are all worth it. Risks are not for lazy people, but for those with a passion for their mission.

God's Game Plan is exciting, and it is important to know this plan and pass it along to your team and others. After all, which is more important—"your game" or "God's Game"?

Pursuit:

1. Am I settling for "status quo," or am I taking the responsibility to go to the next level?

2. Is my horse dead; is it time to dismount?

Week 49

Commitments

Game Plan:
2 Timothy 2:2

Challenge:

Leaders should continually make commitments and set goals.

Coach Bill McCartney once spoke at an FCA event and challenged everyone there to make a commitment to accountability. We all need accountability. It is too easy to fall. God's Word says we must build one another up continuously. We all need a small group that we can be transparent with, encourage, and speak the truth in love.

What commitments do you need to make?

1. Begin a daily quiet time with God.
2. Begin a regular Bible study.
3. Stop cheating your family by spending too much time at work.
4. Save money.
5. Give money.
6. Share Christ with your team and fellow coaches.
7. Begin an exercise and better eating program.
8. Raise the level of leadership skills you have.

9. Quit living in the past, and concentrate on making a difference now.

10. Focus more on people rather than things.

Pursuit:

1. Do I have an accountability partner? If not, find one.

2. List your commitments. Be realistic, and be accountable to someone about them.

LaVergne, TN USA
24 January 2010
170991LV00002B/1/P